human
verses

poems by

katya zinn

Finishing Line Press
Georgetown, Kentucky

human
verses

For Will.

Why can't we see
the whole of anything
until the hole

it leaves behind?
I told you ask again in two years
but you only lived one more.

& I don't know if this is
a dedication or a poem
but Will, this is for you

for everything you saw
& everything you showed me;

we'll get it right in the next life.
And I'm sorry I never said
it while it mattered

but I did.
and I do.

and I Will.

ACKNOWLEDGMENTS

Thank you to James Merenda, Lip Manegio, and Brandon Melendez for your
words and Renata Watson for your photos.
Thank you to Zoetic and Storm of Blue Press for publishing earlier drafts of
'umbrella dreamscapes (an odyssey)' and 'Anniversary syndrome.'
Thank you Aby, for giving my book such a wonderful cover, and me such a
wonderful friendship.
Thank you to my family.

Publisher: Leah Huete de Maines
Editor: Christen Kincaid
Cover Art and Design: Aby Normal
Author Photo: Renata Watson

Printed in the USA on acid-free paper.
Order online: www.finishinglinepress.com
            also available on amazon.com

Author inquiries and mail orders:
Finishing Line Press
P. O. Box 1626
Georgetown, Kentucky 40324
U. S. A.

Contents

human

human

vs.

simulacrum

A cult leader once told me a tornado
can change direction, but never its nature.
Meteorologically speaking, I'm not sure this is a fact

but it feels too true
not to be one.

If you've ever seen a Denny's ad
you probably saw bubbling dish-soap
spooned over cold soy sauce;
mistook it for freshly-poured coffee

which implies the existence
of an alternate universe

where matter dwells
in speculative perfection
untouched by time,

or entropy—
an effervescent forever
technicolor daydream

beside which even reality
appears too dull and lackluster

to be convincingly itself.

the creature in your place

Something's eating away
in the foundations

of the first place I've dared to
in some time   call Home.

This is not a metaphor.
the building inspector says we have a very serious problem
with squirrels.

When glass shatters,
can you tell which piece
the others
were pieces of?

A friend says survival is a choice
to kill or forgive
the creature left in your place

there once was a man with a beautiful wife he locked in a yellow room in a
yellow house by the sea and she tore the yellow paper from the yellow walls
till her hands bled red because there were people inside them she said they
whispered while she slept she said she had to set them all free—

it's another kind of funny
how everyone remembers that story
for the wallpaper-people
not the curtains, or the sound of the sea
can you remember something
that doesn't exist?

~~which piece do you blame~~
~~for the mess?~~

when there's nothing left to hold
when your handle breaks
can you solace yourself
in soap-bubble daydream? is forever only fiction? can you tell
warmth from salt? have you taken
the eye of a storm   for stillness?
can you forgive the creature in your place

who played your part so well
you show up not-bubbly enough   to be convincingly
yourself?

The squirrels are chewing through walls now.
There was one on my pillow
this morning, I swear, when I woke.
What do you owe to the creature in your place?

which piece is the one
that broke?

It happened, I swear. I saw it. I was there
but the squirrel in my bed doesn't stay for the camera
gone in a twitch of tail before I lift the lens

but not before he sees me
see him

& how I seemed to him then so human
so lousy in design,
furnishing evidence
for what my senses already knew
the way he glanced back before

leaving, as though to say
Go ahead, tell them.

Tell anyone you like how you woke
to my face below yours in that bed.

Tell them, and see who believes you.

Anniversary syndrome

Arianna says I'd die first in a horror movie / always scouring darkness for night-bumping sounds / ripe with mortal curiosity

/

so I had tea with a cult leader on Friday, I mention / in a car packed with people I love / Myles calls this on-brand / which I call being Seen / when clinking teacups with High Priest of the Church of Euthanasia falls / somewhere in the scope / of Shit I Can be Expected to Do.

/

every fall I spiral like the dying leaves on balding branches / *seasonal triggers,* my therapist calls this / ptsd's never sounded so festive / couples pick apples off my forearms / my skin bleeds pumpkin spice

/

it's fall in first grade & I'm Star of the Week / filling in an All About Me for the bulletin board / *what are you scared of?*

/

I read a tweet once that said *My childhood taught me quicksand would be a bigger problem* / I couldn't relate

/

this fall I teach a first-grader named Eva who's unfazed by the undead / *I'll use my Zombie Sword,* she says. *Duh.* / & from her I learn Fear is just / a byproduct / of lacking a specific enough Sword for an imminent threat

/

my brother points to a swampy bit of stream / *that's quicksand,* he says / obviously, I need to verify this myself

/

grocery list: october
•   Quicksand Sword

- Sword of Falls Past
- 'I-Carve-Myself-Up-Like-a-Porchtop-Pumpkin-for-People-Who-Would-Not-do-the-Same-for-me-&-I-Don't-Know-Whether-to-Call-This-Compassion-or-Masochism' Sword
- 'I'm-a-Shitty-Role-Model-Because-I-Forge-my-Responsibility-to-be-a-Role-Model-for-my-Students-into-a-Personal-'Latent-Need-to-Self-Destruct-Sword' Sword

/

paper jack-o-lanterns smile toothless on the walls in room 13 / *what are you afraid of?* / justin said zombies & tracey put ghosts / my head says *nothing* / but I don't want mrs. lantz to think I'm a poser / I write *I am scared of pumpkins with scary faces*

A more self-aware six-year-old might have written
I am so scared my lack of self-preservative instincts are already distancing me from relationships I value, I desecrated the Star of the Week board with lies.

/

Anniversary syndrome is a lot like being stuck in quicksand / the outside world takes the shape of swallowing you whole / loving someone you shouldn't is a lot like living next to the leader of a death cult / theoretically dangerous but you always walk away with a story

/

jackie was afraid of the top of the jungle-gym / I watch the city from rooftops just to feel / the abyss beneath my feet / my therapist calls this *high-risk behavior* / I call it

fearing for my life is the fastest way of remembering I want to live

/

it's the fog of a dying september & I'm at my first college party / I climb the rocks outside because I can / before the fall I am young & drunk & invincible

/

before he was a haunting he was just a boy I texted at night;
hey can u come to my room im scared

/

I am five or six & my body's never been this high up before / air tastes thin &
sticky in my throat / I look down at my father / a towering speck at the end of
his rope / tell him *I'm done climbing now*

No, he says. *You're not at the top yet.*

/

my therapist says *This is not what I meant*
when I asked if you remember a time you were scared

when someone you loved
did not let you down.

Experiment: operant conditioning in rats

METHODS
- rats press lever
- receive food pellet

Control variable—continuous reward
Results—rats get bored
Add **independent variable**
- call it x
- randomly replace reward with electric shock.

Results
- fat rats mash lever
- fried little rat brains get hooked (on intermittent reinforcement).

ABSTRACT

The way you loved me, you said it made you lose control. But for me! for me, you would try (to do *better*, to be *better*; because I deserved *better*). And I— stuffed my cheeks with those words; until I had no room to speak. Because letting myself break meant failing; at fixing you. You see, the most dangerous part (about electrocution) is not the pain. It's the convulsions[1]

BACKGROUND

Electrocution
Victims lose agency over physiological responses, must be pried free from sources, and still, subjects reported they stayed, "for the nourishment."
Electrocution Victims
will tell you Pain was a choice, because it means at least they still had one[2]

CONCLUSIONS
Guilt
proves the laws of entropy. We've observed how it slides / through blood-slick hands, and settles / in empty places—in hands searching, reaching for something (anything) to hold onto, like a lever.
Or hard data, behind every unrecorded

No. You
can always spot a lab rat

---

1 the biological glitch that makes living limbs involuntarily contract around deadly, charged objects
2 even with the every Viscera cooked ashen by current, will still look you in the eyes with theirs rolled flat-white and say *the real shock...is we ever believed we deserved to be fed.*

by the claw marks
in everything
they have to let go[3]

DISCUSSION

I still think about those rats, often
and when I do, I wonder
if they just went back to leading their little rat lives after
pretending nothing had changed, or

if leverless, they grew listless
purposeless
if they ever chewed
on live wires
just to know they were
alive, &
what about the aftershocks?

long after the experiment's finished
does the voltage
still keep them awake?
do their still-charged neurons dance

between clarity
   & conditioning
stuck in circuitry
       never settling
never solving
       for that forever
elusive variable

it's not the x;
       that's long gone now.

it's *y*

    ?

---

3 I never noticed
how close love was to fear
until I realized I didn't know
the difference.

dermatillomania

I do not want to write this poem about my hands.
I do not want to write this poem
about never knowing what to do with my hands.

as a child, I learned to braid
my fingers together before my hair
wrung to claws by daybreak
 till there was no moving them—
on those nights,
I'd wake to my own scream.

when I got older but not old enough
I hid screams in empty brown bottles with the paper
peeled off / fingernail staccato on the creases
of red plastic cups, till those restless hands, one night
woke to someone else
moving them
(this time,
I could not scream.)

I will not be saved
from de-gloving my hands
by poem or by silly putty:
I know the first step

towards breaking a habit
is understanding its function, but if you hand me
a relevant worksheet, I'll probably just bleed on it.

The more you tear away the same skin, the harder it grows back
the deeper you have to dig to find softness, but I've seen it -
give me a half hour in a waiting room
or Netflix and a pair of tweezers; it's there

in rusty trails on the corners of my textbooks
I know read the same as self-harm
    but consider:

Every seven years, the human epidermis regenerates its every cell from scratch.

Someday, I'll be made of skin
his hands have never touched
but until then, is it such a harm
to scratch it out from under this one?

like cracking open a Geode
like carving up a rough draft & finding
a perfect poem;
there *is* a poem
inside these hands, but I do not want to write it

& yet until I do, it becomes gravity in my bones
pins me to a prison of sheets
    so I will write this poem

about the time my friend Geo
did a stick-n-poke a constellation
on the back of my right hand & asked why it
didn't hurt. I will write this poem

about losing objects I'm still holding
because my mind & body are exes
with a break-up so painful they can't be
in the same room yet.

I will write this poem
about ashtrays & inkpads
about orange peels & pincushions & everything else
I've turned these hands into
just to prove they were still mine.
            and.
I will write this poem

about everything these hands can do
without destroying themselves,
like petting dogs
showing cat-callers both my middle fingers
& once
watering a drugstore succulent for six months
before I noticed it was plastic
& for three nights after

as a grown-up who knew better but still held fast to the hope
that *lifeless once doesn't mean forever dead*

just imagine
when this body finally catches
up to its head
all the time I'll grow
& imagine, then

how I'll cradle these raw, open hands of mine in each other
like wounded birds
& I'll say *forgive me, little ones*
for these hurts of mine I made you wear.
It's not your fault; I'm sorry; you're safe.
You're safe,
and we're going home now.

We're going home.

human

-verses

Brief Interviews with Higher Selves
after David Foster Wallace

Have you ever had a moment like that, though?

Q.

Where it's like this invisible veil is peeled back and all of a sudden you're there, you know? Wedged right in that moment. Not regretting the ones before it, not dreading the ones after. It's like coming alive again, like a little rebirth, and all the colors are brighter somehow, like you've only seen in black-and-white until now. Everything's thrown into this dazzling high-definition, and you'd swear you could count the cells in every blade of grass, or the leaves on every tree, and you're just like, suddenly, intimately aware of the fact that they're alive, and you're alive too. You know?

Q.

I don't get very many of those moments, I guess. I don't get very many moments at all.

Q.

Meaning I don't ever experience things as they happen. I have emotion the way wax-paper left too long in the rain eventually grows soggy. Everything just glances off this coating of numbness and horror and boredom. The bad stuff just weighs me down more than I really feel it. More than I recognize it as one specific, situationally-appropriate emotion. And the good things, they aren't persistent enough to inspire a change of state. But sometimes, without warning, it happens, and it's like I see into an entirely new universe; see what life could be if I was ever free from this.

Q.

I dunno, whatever it is that puts everything in shades of pain and less pain. Like having stencils over your eyes all the time.

Q.

The best way I can explain it is if you pay attention to people's stories, there's certain archetypes of abuser that start to show up across the board, right? And it's like, if it happens enough times everything becomes an archetype, until eventually you're subconsciously casting people in this, like, cyclical reenactment of your own trauma. You can try to ignore it, you can try to stuff it down, but until you deal with it you're gonna keep reliving it. Sometimes in ways that aren't even happening outside of your head.

Q.

I get distracted looking for short-term fixes, I think. Maybe that's the problem, though, seeing myself as something to be Fixed? I dunno. But I'd forgotten what happiness felt like until that first line. Then suddenly it was like, *is this how normal people feel all the time? Is this what it's like to be happy?*

Q.

Like, if there was a parallel universe where The Incident never happened, like Me from that universe and whoever, whatever I've become in response, are fighting for control over one body.

Q.

Right, but that's what happiness is, I think. I mean, clearly I'm not like, well-versed in the concept, but I feel like it's—I mean—none of that disappears, right? It's just that in the moment it's swallowed by something greater. This fantastical awareness of infinite possibility, you know?

Q.

I'm talking about the Now. This. Like, this whole time I've been looking for a future I could tolerate my own existence in, or some kind of closure about the past so I could stop living there, but it turns out the whole time the answer was—well, not right in front of me, but exactly where I was standing.

Q.

Now. That's it. The Present. It's funny, I guess it's what people had been trying to get me to see for so long, through like, mindfulness, meditation, yoga, all that shit I used to say was just crunchy-granola nonsense Neurotypicals used to sell self-help books.

Q.

So there was this one night on the road trip last summer, where we rolled up in Myrtle Beach at like four in the morning, and we had nowhere to sleep for what was left of the night, and, I mean I've never been super comfortable with y'know, (sweeping gestures from head to thighs) the whole Meat-suit part of the deal, but this time, for whatever reason I just went fuck it, and stripped. First one to do it. And we all sprinted into the Atlantic, and for once I wasn't thinking how I ate too much trail mix, or how I wasn't journaling enough, or, like, hyper-focusing on some mundane Flesh-prison flaw. We were just bodies in the night, delirious with our own freedom, hurtling towards victory, or disaster, maybe both. But it didn't matter, because right then that was all there was.

Q.

It's just there's so few things that take up my entire brain capacity, you know? There's a darkness in the corners and I've gotten alright at quarantining it, but I didn't believe in the Quiet until I heard it for the first time. I didn't believe in anything. But I believe in it now.

Q.

No, not like a god or even any specific spirituality, just…moments.

Q.

I do. I believe in moments. And that's enough for now.

theories of the humanverse

let's talk about quantum physics. let's talk about
things that only matter when they're measured
like particles & waves
& abandonment.

let's talk about my father
a man who has (on three occasions) yelled at me
for not believing he is proud of me
and said the words *I am proud of you*
on zero.

let's talk about parallel universes.
let's talk about decisions
& indecisions
& how each one we make
or don't make / splinters this cosmic now
into infinite
& equally probable / realities. let's talk about

all these dimensions of ourselves,
the ones together
& the ones still searching
for a love that's
both salvation and ruin
until we find out which.
let's talk

about gravity.
let's talk about this
inexplicable attraction, this
magnetic madness, this need

to bury every piece of myself in-
side you, stich you up & then
sew shut the fabric
of a universe
you can never leave.
let's call *that* gravity.
not love;
call it the intergalactic forces
of shared possibility, reaching

pulling lonely planets
across a vac-
uum of uncertainty
searching   for symmetry.
let's talk about nuclear fission.
let's talk about our first lesson that splitting
creates un-

stable parts
& all the ways we find
not to listen, because even now

when I'm still finding
fragments of my-
self on your shoelaces, I know
none of us are really one person

we are all   entire universes.

concentric structures of decisions & indecisions & parallel planes of planetary
possibility pressed between particles destined   for collision.let's stop
calling it mental illness

& start calling it extra-
terrestrial sensing   this ability to contain infinities
                                    of alternate selves &
      their alternate worlds inside the solar system of a skull.
                        let's talk about how I
      both loathed and envied your   singularity of systems
                        the way they all / revolved
            around a uniformity of self I   have never known.
                              let's talk about how I tried

aligning mine by joining your orbit.   let's talk about how it
                                    almost worked.

let's talk about wormholes & blackholes & infinite ways to lose yourself
in a timeless wasteland of what might have been.   let's talk
      about poetry.

& what a volatile science it is to expand word into w o r l ds we will never inhabit.

let's talk about thomas young
first to discover light   behaves differently when observed
& galen strawson   first to speculate consciousness itself
                                 lends matter physical form
& finally   this poet
                                 possibly first to extrapolate that may-

be, it is only our certainty   in the capacity of things
to remain themselves
that allows them   to occupy space   across
infinite   possible   realities.
for instance,

let's talk about yesterday, over breakfast
when i asked again if you were intending to stay

& just like that
you vanished.

let's talk about entanglement
(quantum or otherwise)
& how, in all the ways I told my-
self you would save me, letting me go

was the last one
I could ever

have predicted.

umbrella dreamscapes (an odyssey)

We're not going to make it.

I am not testing you, my love

(stealing slivers of your smile
through this jar of kitchen door)

I am here to immortalize gratitude
in bullet-points, hollow-points
shrapnel blossoms
beneath my skin
to list as gift this unstained evening
before it becomes
our last.

Daylight leaves a ghost called shadow
the spitting faucet puddles by the window
and if I lit the dark for you at all
maybe it was only blinking
lights aboard midnight vessels
crossing the same oil-slick oceans. My love,

I am much more wreck than ship.
Wasted lifetimes chasing sirens, my insides splintered holes, and still
 I stayed afloat with just a bucket
boat to sea   sea to boat   and back again
I knew nothing more of sailing
       than Sisyphean exchange of salt
                    until the first time you held me
and though I thought I might break apart in your hands,   for once
nothing on the inside
 was leaking

     but you were always first to see the rocks
and o the damage we did that night
                              in such different desperations
choreographed disaster, slow-motion shatter
                    we fought and then fucked and then fought again.
You took my nightclothes
off with my bearings as I rolled over-
board; waves like liquid umbrellas waxed rhythmic return: *all is lost;*

it's your fault, your fault, and I, even in my emptiest delusion
could've called it nothing more
    than at best,
    a reckless
            Almost.

We're not going to make it.

We were young and scarred and scared
traded shards and tried
to walk away with clean hands
like burying ourselves in each other
        could ever make us whole
like we could hold onto flame
            without becoming ashes
matchbox children
            fire-blind and fingers burnt
whatever we had, it was brief
    destructive
            smaller than its own shadow
but for a soap bubble's
    eternity
            it kept us warm.

So I raked my nails down your back like living people do
        your forehead against mine, your smile, and I forgot
all the hands I'd outlasted this lifetime by turning to stone;
you were the only one to keep me
inside a body while on top of it
                        the only one I opened my eyes for
until you pushed your palms against my shoulders

laced your fingers through mine where they lay
                upon your cheek, sucked them clean
of a tenderness never mine to give you; your eyes closed
        teeth grazing
                        my knuckles; I knew
        I wasn't the face
under your eyelids, but a question
mark on your head-board; retreat from Limbo
        to the second circle of Inferno, never your Calypso, and you

19

were still lost
on her island behind lashes, spade-stirred dirt, your nightstand gaslamp—
homes you've never left, and yet she cannot
        stray from, and none of us
            it seems, ever learned
                        much about letting go.

    But two of us still can
            at least one I promise Will
and even so and after still to you (on Styx) I swear: *if I could trade, my love*

I would for you. I'd take those lonely places as my own if I could for you;
bring back to earth
                        everything it took from you; never felt so close
and still so distant, so certain and uncertain:
so big and yet so small.
Never saw the dream for what it was until it was no more
but it did always seem
too natural to be more than simulation
            incubation of hushed comfort stolen
while you slept; your friends
            were like my own. In this life or the next, one said once to me
I've never met someone who loves
quite as selflessly as you do. And this I wish I could keep at least

    but it would be a lie
    there is no sacrifice in loving
                        nothing so much
                                    as making you happy
            and nothing so little
                        as drowning

We're not going to make it

here, on this countertop where you found me
my smile splintered wood between my cheeks
your footsteps cotton comfort at the doorway
and I realized my mistake:
            it was never my abyss to reach into

and outside's just as jarring

just as full of noisy strangers
as this party I fled
to perch beside this dripping faucet
and be as broken as I dare.

I cannot begrudge you your umbrella
while clinging to my bucket
and until the water claims us all

we've earned the right to choose
our private acts of pretending

so forgive me, my love
for I was so full of buoyant hope

and so very,
very stupid.

the science of losing things

four weeks the sky   hung error-screen grey
    husked like empty   chapstick
                              (or how i'd imagine it)   to
look, though always lost too soon
to know what Balm   might look like spent
            & spent too many   loose-change hours
pondering the archetypal energy of exposed fire escapes
the blue halo of a cigarette / elbows' nest of a window-ledge / past-life lovers
                              I've come to both love & fear
the way sleepless nights curl
                back the edges of the world like parchment
                        embers / embryos / embalmings
telephones, wallets, sun   -dry bits of sense
                        disappear into the nothing below.
most lost things, I'm the last place I'd look
until the moon went missing
(vanished for a spell, from the squat of night
above the tenement stack across the street)
                        and but for the fuss I struck
I think no one would   have noticed.
a theory of quantum physics likens the observable universe
to a holographic projection of the mind
            which if true, stands to reason
                would be susceptible, like any simulation, to gl/tch
no one is as sane as they think they are.
 at least once, we all sacrifice our senses
at the altar of belief
bow before personal delusions   of normalcy.
how long do you think it would take the world to notice if the moon stopped
appearing at night?
                no one is as sane as they think they are
                        but jude from across-the-street
by the moonless tenement stack
                    has smiling eyes & speaks to james
in creole on our porch-step
            & he never waves me off with talk of weather
texts my phone one foggy night like verse
                    like a prophecy—
I look for your moon, dear;
she hides.

a spell to conjure wholeness

once, I discovered the secrets of the universe at my kitchen table
                                                but they were too big
for the hole
                        at the back of my skull.
                        once, I was born
soft & full of wonder
a lump of clay in the hands
of a child / michelangelo once said   he did not carve david

but released him from marble.
        Listen.
                can you tell silence from the absence of voices?

                        can you prove it
                        exists?
                                can you prove
i cannot hold silence
                in my fist ?
                if a tree falls in the woods with no body to witness

does it pick itself up
and try again ?

can you prove
boundaries of skin anymore real   than a hand slicing air?
        i do not have arrogance enough to call this poem *mine*
i have no proof i wrote it   that it wasn't already in the air here
on the bend of on a midnight highway / the silence between two lovers
                                                        Listen.
                        *

god is love is god is love is god is love is god is love is god is love is god

                        *

child of earth, can you prove you are not perfect?
                                that silence exists?
that the breaking of silence is not
the opening of a fist?

            you astral flower, you starseed-spacedust-spaceship

you miracle
you cannot be mended
you weren't broken to begin with

you headlight sunset, you sun-soak daydream, you brave explorer on this
quest of today—
i must tell you, though it hurts
to heavy your load with truth—
the promise of healing from loss
is a myth
we are all shaped by absence
from our first breath on the earth
the way the air in your lungs once was shaped
like the spaces between things
but the greatest myth of all is absence

makes less than a whole
that love unreturned
is love lost or wasted
there is no beginning or end
to the line of a circle
there is no me or you
to the eyes of beyond
one day we will all cease to be something
& become part of everything
but it's not for you to decide when that is.

can you prove you're alone by yourself? can you prove you *are* yourself?
can you prove yourself to you?
and if you are
and if you have
and if you can
then tell me
how right now
you have my voice
in your head?

human

after the third attempt

my brother
wrote my parents a letter I found
on the top shelf of their credenza
the night before Christmas this year. It ended:

I hope things go back to normal soon, or
as normal as it ever gets with her.

it's been three years now
since our last family reunion
took place around my hospital bed; three years, since I last lost
a staring contest to the abyss, and still

each day feels like another line / etched
on a prison wall, another scratch
            between today
            & the last day
            I tried to make
            my last
            & I guess
that's about as normal as it ever gets with me

but isn't that
a kind of victory?
to stare down all that once tried to destroy you
& say look what I have built   on rubble.
Look at all this beautiful time   I have stacked
like broken matchsticks; look how I have reached
   with one foot buried six feet deep
   & maybe, maybe it isn't much

but there are mountains taller than everest
when you start on the ocean floor;
there are prisons that don't look like prisons

until you try to open the door;
there are cracks in the sidewalk
with flowers blooming in their place;
crossing the finish line
is not the meaning of the human race;
our lives are not lifeless; this life is
not meant to be sprinted:
this life is a dash—
a dash carved
between two numbers on a gravestone
& maybe putting down my chisel
is about as normal as it gets for me

but fuck their normal.

survival
is an act of defiance

from the very first cell that said *not this time*,
to you, still scanning crowds for an exit sign:
You are not a mistake

even on the days your smile feels
like shards of glass in your cheeks;
when your heart
aches like a missing tooth
& if you still have pill bottles marked *just in case*
if you've ever bled
for the sake of distraction, because distraction
is the closest you ever get to peace; if pain
is the only reason you know you're still living
& the only reason you're still living
is to save others pain
& if that
is as normal as it ever gets for you, then Friend!

I am proud to know you
to know in the time
this line
speaks itself into memory, you

& I, are one, here— an instant eternity; Now
in this realm
of everything uncertain but the possibility
that perception
& pain
are only matters
of matter observing itself

because despite our own best efforts
we are still here
& we do not owe the world an apology
but a purpose

so You, put down that chisel
& You
plant seeds in every sidewalk
& You
never lose hope that something will grow; lord,
if I don't know that it's not easy
but nothing sacred ever is; Friend,

I can't promise you it will get better
but I can promise
that you are not alone.

A brief history of men I don't know offering unsolicited opinions on my life

I.

Lizard Lounge, 10pm.
Man in Cowboy Hat says
I need to date a guy with sisters
says my poems make it sound
as though all men are created Evil.

When he was a boy
(hardly as high as his
ornamental desert-themed belt buckle)
this old man's sisters taught him to braid their hair
& as they did, wove into him their strength, and something
else…I confess, at this point
I stopped listening.

Man in Cowboy Hat says he can solve all my problems with men.

My problem with men is
their standards for acceptable behavior are so low
that biological probability passes as an asset.

My problem with men is I spent four sleepless nights
burning midnight-oil before bluelight, bleeding
words from old scars
like a medieval doctor a ghost of the blood
in the hopes of a poem
one person might hear and feel seen by
but a man in a cowboy hat watched that stage
and saw a missing piece
of a hypothetical man I've never met
that he, a man I just met, decided
could finally fix me.

Forgive me, Mr. Urban Cowboy
if you thought yourself owed softness, but
at exactly zero points

did I ask your opinion
& these jagged edges

match the corners
of boxes I'm shoved in

so don't you dare mistake survival
for broken-ness.

II.

Campus Public Safety, 8pm
Man with a Badge says

you better think twice, little girl
about what you say next
unless you're trying to get someone under arrest

Is it my intention, he asks
to ruin *the rest of a young man's life?*

What about the rest of my life?
No one knows softness
like a thief in the night.

Hands can bruise, and break, and grope
and take, and braid hair too.

But the man with the badge does not ask what his hands did.
The man with the badge asks how much pot I smoke.

Flips his notebook open
like a nightclub stranger
& leaves the pages blank.

How can you be sure
you really know what happened? he asks
& of course, men with pens have always
rewritten the past.

Isn't that why
they called it history?

open letter to the r*pist who writes about MeToo

When you interviewed the woman you made a career on
did you tell her you believed her?

& when you blasted that reporter for planting a false accusation
to sow seeds of doubt, did it remind you
of your own secret garden?

Did you see my face   in the whites of her eyes?
Did you laugh when she told you   what it feels like to die?
what it feels like to be the car   instead of the driver?
Did you call her   a survivor?

or did you call her a liar?   a child?   a victim
of psychosis?   an insane   insecure
shit-stirring   grudge-holding   misguided
misandrist   bitch?

I told you   you made me feel safe.
You asked if I wanted to take my clothes off.

Do you have any idea
how to explain to somebody who only wants to love you
that your biggest trigger
is safety?

hold a mirror in front of a mirror   and it becomes a hall of infinite
reflections   within   reflections
and   between   them
   gaps   within   gaps   within   gaps   and
I carried this poem for two years before I wrote it
because I got stuck in that hallway
& what a hollow kind of lonely it is
when your trauma stops being relatable
when it's too narrow a shard of mirror
for anyone to see themselves in. See,
I once thought myself fluent in comparative language
but there's no metaphor in any language I know
with weight enough to explain how it feels
reading testimony against Brett Kavanaugh
by way of the words of the man who used
his way with words

to get himself off
without charges, after using my body
to get himself off
while my mind
severed itself at the spinal cord
& the cost
of treating dissociative symptoms
is more than I can afford & still less
than he makes for stories
people read when he writes them, but
when I lived them, no one listened
or even cared at all.

Davis,
if this ever gets back to you, I know
you'll convince everyone who matters
in less time than it took to write it
that this is a revenge poem,
but you're wrong. This isn't about revenge.
I swear, I would've shut my mouth while you smirked at me
beside every byline from here to Brooklyn before I told them what you
were, but then—

I told you
you made me feel safe
and you said
Me, too.

& then you made sure I never would be again.
& then, you took the one thing I had without your handprints
& wrote your name across the top
& you're wrong.
This isn't about revenge. It never was. This
is about you, once again
forcing yourself where you do not belong, and I swear—
I swear—to every vengeful God
I stopped believing in that this time—this time

you will not get away with it.

on community, Catan, episodes, & the multiverse

Even Settlers of Catan can become a dissociative episode
when you think too much about parallel universes.

It's your turn. Roll the dice

& observable reality fractals into factorials of probable infinities
at each juncture of their shuddered stillness.
In a season 6 episode of *Community*, the gang lets a die decide
who must answer the door for the pizza guy
& we, the audience, watch each alternate timeline
expand into a parallel universe

In the episode I'm experiencing, I am the die
& the audience
& the spaces between this universe
& the ones where safety still has meaning & I can occupy a room
without positioning myself in sight of every doorway.

Roll nine.

It's not your turn.
Why are you holding the dice?
Time's missing since two turns ago—what have you done?
Responsibility outranks recollection.

You need sheep.
Who has sheep? You asked that already.
You can't love & trust anyone at the same time.
Roll ten.
Probability says you're dead than alive
in more universes where you've existed.
In this one, you're safe; you're with people who love you
but not for long if you keep acting insane.

Shut up. Someone's talking.
When did words stop making sense?
Roll six. Collect sheep.
Did somebody ask you a question?
You need sleep
or a smoke

or maybe just a drink of water.
In a parallel universe you don't believe in parallel universes

never watched yourself split at the seams of dimensions.
Roll eight.
Someone's speaking.
They're waiting on your answer
but you're stuck between realities
like a deck of cards
fanning out in every direction.

Take the hand you were dealt.
It was years ago / it was yesterday / it was your fault—no, it wasn't that bad.
Focus
on the face in front of you. It's real. Like a photograph
in high-definition, but there's spots
like little black holes furling in from the edges.
How long have you been silent? Say something.
Wipe the absence from your face. Say sorry.
Make a joke; make excuses. Make. Words. With. Your. Mouth.
Don't say where you went or they'll take away Outside again.
You know how it happens.
A look sideways, a phone call, a form
that's all it takes for the click of the lock. Don't forget
the way one black hole can condense
every universe to contain you & the voids in between
down a single fluorescent hallway.

In the episode I'm referencing
the dice turns out to be a ruse
Jeff uses to stay in the safety of his chair
& remove himself from the odds by rolling.
In the episode I'm experiencing, I've removed myself
without leaving my chair, because safety
is a ruse I won't roll the odds on

& I'm so tired of this writing itself into everything I write
but the last time felt the safety of home
next to someone I loved, that person made a choice
that splintered my matter of being
into universes called Before & After

& I don't know who I am if not broken
if not stuck
at this event horizon of might-have-been
& trust is a game of chance I never learned the rules of

but I know Erich
eats the same everything bagel for breakfast every morning
with cheese on one half, peanut butter on the other
& James wears Randi's slippers at night
& gestures with his entire body
& Randi laughs like cotton candy sizzling on a stovetop
& Emil has the kind of energy
that makes everyone want to be themselves & be better at the same time

& there's rainbow twinkle lights on the chandelier in the living room
& sculptures made of garbage dangling from the stairwell
& we're settled in Catan
at 3am on a Wednesday, like nothing else matters
& time is a circular gameboard populated by pieces
who pretend for fun they call the shots

but no one at this table is a stranger
to the snakes and ladders of playing, so

Trust.
It's your turn.

Roll the dice.

Acknowledgments

There are many people and places I want to thank, without whom this book would not exist in its current form. In no particular order…

Thank you to Emil Eastman (without whom I'd have neither Haus nor home) for their coaching, friendship, endless support, and occasional curbside treasures.

Thank you to Alex Charalambides, for believing in this 'whole heart of a book,' and helping coax my galaxy brain into executive functioning.

Thank you to my White Haus family for all the joy, laughter, inspiration, and community.

Speaking of community, thank you to Slam Free or Die and Boston Poetry Slam for helping me grow as a poet, and more importantly as a human being.

Thank you to Mason Granger, for booking my very first gig as a featured poet, and for showing me warmth, welcome, and the best bagels in Brooklyn, and to Julius Boltonado, for making said first gig possible by hosting me, and helping me.

Thank you to Myles Taylor—friend, younger parental figure, and occasional bionic coach, and all of Team Amateur Hour (Sam, Sarah, Kenn), for all your support, inspiration, and belief in the wild dream of sending our tiny school's first team to the national stage.

Thank you to Sarah Purnell, for showing me endless encouragement, compassion, and unconditional love throughout the seven years I've been blessed to call you my friend, and for sitting through the seven entire minutes of angsty rambling that doubled as the first draft of my first spoken-word poem.

Thank you to Anna and Jack Dalrymple, without whom I undoubtedly would not have survived long enough to write this.

Born and raised in Southern California, **Katya Zinn** is the black-sheep child of two scientists. She graduated summa cum laude from Lesley University in 2019 where she majored in Expressive Art Therapy, minored in Global Studies, and captained her school's first team to compete on the national stage at the College Union Poetry Slam Invitational. She is the winner of the July Silver Needle Press award for Creative Nonfiction. Her work has been featured in *Underground, Merrimack Review, Silver Needle Press,* and *Where the Mind Dwells*. Zinn is the founder of the Paper Doll Project, a multimedia exhibit focused on art by and for survivors of gender-based violence, for which she won the 2019 Selase Williams Social Activism Through the Arts award. As a Title IX educator and activist, she is a legislative advocate for the Every Voice Coalition to End Campus Sexual Violence and leads consent education workshops for college students. Currently, she works with children with multiple disabilities at Perkins School for the Blind in Watertown, Massachusetts, and is preparing for an upcoming Fulbright fellowship to teach English and the craft of spoken word poetry in rural Malaysian communities. Her work focuses on the power of storytelling as a means of social change, personal growth, and intercultural understanding. She also has a side hustle as a freelance dream interpreter and probably wants to be your friend. For bookings or to follow her work please find her on Twitter and Instagram at @zinnvisibleink.

CPSIA information can be obtained
at www.ICGtesting.com
Printed in the USA
LVHW091721170521
687652LV00026B/1419

9 781646 624461